BASKETBALL HALL OF FAMERS

OSCAR ROBERTSON

Joel H. Cohen

rosen
central

To Art W. and Ed M., all-star lovers of the game

Published in 2002 by The Rosen Publishing Group, Inc.
29 East 21st Street, New York, NY 10010

First Edition

Library of Congress Cataloging-in-Publication Data

Cohen, Joel H.
Oscar Robertson / by Joel H. Cohen.
p. cm. — (Basketball Hall of Famers)
Includes bibliographical references (p.) and index.
Summary: A biography of the professional basketball player, nicknamed the "Big O," who overcame poverty and racism to become what some consider the best all-around player of all time.
ISBN 0-8239-3485-3 (library binding)
1. Robertson, Oscar, 1938-—Juvenile literature. 2. Basketball players—United States—Biography—Juvenile literature.
[1. Robertson, Oscar, 1938– 2. Basketball players. 3. African Americans—Biography.]
I. Title. II. Series.
GV884.R6 C64 2001
796.323'092—dc21   *0/00 – 62860 mm*

                                                    2001003210

Manufactured in the United States of America

contents

Introduction

While different professional basketball players have excelled at different skills, such as shooting, passing, or rebounding, Oscar Robertson mastered them all.

An outstanding leader and athlete, he overcame poverty, racism, and substandard practice facilities, outplaying highly talented opponents in high school, college, and professional competition, to become what some consider the greatest all-around basketball player of all time.

College all-star, all-American, Olympian, National Basketball Association champion, and Hall of Famer, the Big O—as Robertson was admiringly known—set hard-to-match records throughout the 1960s and built a reputation for greatness that has lasted to this day.

Oscar Robertson, shown here in his Cincinnati Royals uniform, is widely considered to be the best all-around basketball player in the history of the game.

As to his many accomplishments in basketball, Robertson said on his Web site, http://www.thebigo.com, that no particular one was the most satisfying. "I just got enjoyment out of being able to play and do well at each successive level of competition. That in itself was satisfaction enough."

The Beginnings of a Champion

Oscar Palmer Robertson's fascination with sports began when he started playing basketball at seven years of age. Too poor to own a basketball, he learned how to shoot by tossing a tennis ball or even rags bundled with rubber bands into an empty peach basket.

Later, too, when a real basketball was available, he worked nonstop to sharpen his skills. Larry Ridley, a childhood friend who became a professional jazz musician and college music professor, recalled how Robertson would constantly practice shooting a basketball from morning to night. "He'd go to different parts of the court and just keep working on his shot and release. I knew then this guy was really going to be something."

Echoes from the Schoolyard

This is what basketball gave to me . . . When I was seven or eight years old, where was I? What dreams could I have? People who lived where I did didn't have dreams about anything. They were just living, drifting.

"To have dreams, you have to have your curiosity aroused, to see different things, talk to people about things, read books. I loved to do this. That's how I got into basketball and that's when I started to dream about something else.

—Oscar Robertson

"Echoes from the Schoolyard," 1977, as it appeared in the *Indianapolis Star*, Sunday, June 11, 1989

Looking back on his childhood, Robertson said on NBA.com, "Playing basketball helped me to gain confidence in my life. I also became a better student, because I had a coach who told me I'd have to get better grades or I wouldn't play on his team."

Basketball did something more for Robertson. It helped him grow socially and racially. Because he grew up in a neighborhood

This college photograph of Oscar Robertson captures the University of Cincinnati star player making one of his signature behind-the-back passes.

where he never saw a white person, playing with white athletes was a tremendous experience.

It may also have kept him out of hot water. "I never got into trouble," he told Paul Hemphill in *Sport*, "but the potential was there. A lot of my old buddies went to jail and got messed up in crime."

Robertson was born on November 24, 1938, in rural Charlotte, Tennessee. When he was four years old, he moved with his parents and his two brothers, Bailey and Henry, to Indianapolis, Indiana, where they lived in a segregated housing project.

His grandfather, who read the Bible to Oscar and his brothers every night, had been a slave. Thinking back about his grandfather's experience, Oscar wondered aloud during an NBA Store panel discussion on the Underground Railroad: "Could I have done that? I don't know. It must have been terrible in those days for blacks just to exist."

After the divorce of his mother, a beautician, and his father, a meat packer, Oscar stayed close to both. It was then that Tom

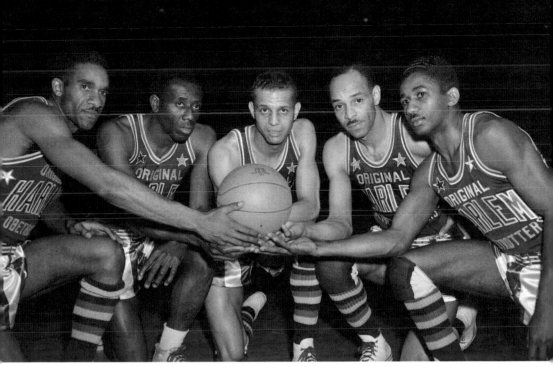

As a young boy, Oscar Robertson was awed by the skills and antics of the Harlem Globetrotters, especially those of Goose Tatum *(second from left)* and Marques Haynes *(far right).*

Sleet, an eighth-grade coach, took him under his wing.

"He was the first major influence in my life. He'd played for Butler University, and he did more for me than I'd ever be able to repay," Robertson said of Sleet, who helped kids both on and off the court.

"Robertson was always a great guy," according to his friend, Larry Ridley. Ridley, in twenty-eight years of teaching music at

Rutgers University, urged his students to employ the same kind of energy, dedication, and commitment to practicing and rehearsing as Oscar did with basketball.

"Oscar always was popular, and very cool and tolerant," Ridley recalled. And unlike so many of the young people he grew up with, Robertson gave the impression of having aspirations, and no one doubted he would achieve them.

Robertson played ball in the local police athletic league, and, in summers, competed with other future basketball stars on his home court, which was known as the Dust Bowl. According to Dan Dunkin, writing in the *Indianapolis Star* in 1989, Robertson believed that that patch of asphalt was no less important than the first peach basket hung by Dr. James Naismith, the inventor of the game.

When asked about his heroes, Robertson said, "We didn't really think in terms of [heroes or] role models in those days. We enjoyed watching the Globetrotters, particularly Marques Haynes and Goose Tatum, so if I had a role model, I guess the Globetrotters would be it."

High School Hero

When it was time for high school, Robertson attended Crispus Attucks High School, named for a heroic runaway slave who was killed in the Boston Massacre preceding the Revolutionary War. Until the early 1950s, it had been the only public school in Indianapolis that African American children were permitted to attend.

Even before Robertson became a student there, he had a rooting interest in its team. In the final seconds of the 1951 regional title game, Robertson's older brother, Bailey "Flap" Robertson, then a five-foot-nine sophomore, hit the shot that gave Attucks High an 81–80 victory over Anderson High School. It was one of the most dramatic moments in Indiana high school tournament history.

Watching his brother's game-winning basket on television, Robertson was inspired—in the words of a Purdue University history professor, Randy Roberts—to what was possible when "basketball and joy, race and achievement come together." The shot may have launched Oscar into his out-of-this-world athletic career.

Remarkably, Attucks High had no gym where its basketball team could practice, and, until Robertson's playing at the school made headlines, the majority of white area schools refused to play Attucks High. But, led by Robertson, the Attucks Tigers achieved tremendous success, and fans packed arenas throughout the state to watch them. Everyone then wanted to play the Tigers.

The team's coach, Ray Crowe, was obsessed with the fundamentals of the sport, and according to the National Basketball Association (NBA), "Robertson smoothly combined his street smarts with Coach Crowe's fundamentals." The coach wouldn't allow his players to dribble behind their backs or dunk the ball. In fact, he threatened that any player who dared play using these moves would be dumped from the team. Talking on the court was also taboo, which is why Robertson seldom spoke during games, even in the pros.

Freshmen were not eligible to play at Attucks High, so it wasn't until the second game of his sophomore year that Robertson started. Once he was in the lineup, he excelled, leading Attucks

This photograph captures Oscar Robertson midair after grabbing a rebound during a game in Manhattan, Kansas, in March 1959.

High to an incredible forty-five game winning streak, a state record, and Indiana state championships in 1955 and 1956. (Losing only one game in two seasons, while winning sixty-two, the team had a record of 31–1 in 1955 and 31–0 in 1956.)

With the 1955 title, Attucks High took home the first state championship won by an Indianapolis team, and it became the first exclusively black school to accomplish that feat. The next year, Attucks High was the first team to win the state crown with an undefeated record.

"I don't think any team in the country could have beaten the team we had at Crispus Attucks," Robertson declared on his Web site.

When asked what he considers the greatest moments in his basketball career, he often cites those championship high school days. His favorite memory from high school basketball, he noted on the same site, was the first championship in 1955. "Nothing else comes close."

Like many other NBA stars, Robertson benefited equally from excellent coaching and self-determination. He always felt that coaching was important, especially during high school. "A good coach not only emphasizes the fundamentals of your sport; he or she also emphasizes the mental aspect of the game and how to play together as a team. You can look at players and tell who had good coaching and who did not," he said on his Web site. "Coaches can give you drills and guidance, but you have to teach yourself," he continued.

Robertson feels people learn to play basketball from those they compete with and by watching other players. The sport itself became his outlet and a daily learning experience.

In three years at Attucks High, Robertson set school scoring records, netting 1,780 points. As a senior, he averaged 24.6 points per game, had a single-game high of 62 points, was named to the high school all-American first team, and was National High School Player of the Year.

As player of the year in 1956, he was given the state's top designation as Indiana's Mr. Basketball and led the Indiana All-Stars to a sweep of the Kentucky All-Stars.

Years later, when the *Indianapolis Star* conducted a poll as part of the fifty-year anniversary of the Indiana All-Star Dream Team, fans elected Robertson the all-time Mr. Basketball. Robertson received 2,161 votes, ahead of George McGinnis (1,709 votes), who in 1969 had led his high school (Indianapolis Washington) to the state championship and later starred at Indiana University and in the NBA.

McGinnis commented in the *Indianapolis Star*, "Oscar was, I think, the best high school basketball player there ever was. And what

Oscar Robertson of the Cincinnati Royals swats the ball away from K.C. Jones during an NBA playoff game against the Boston Celtics on March 31, 1964.

separates him from everybody else is that he was outstanding throughout his playing career, regardless of whether you're talking high school, college, or [the] pros."

It was no surprise when Robertson was elected to both the National High School Basketball Hall of Fame and the Indiana Basketball Hall of Fame.

Indiana has always been a basketball-crazy state, and fans are even fanatical about high school games, so Robertson quickly became a household name.

Future basketball stars Tom and Dick Van Arsdale weren't yet in high school when they watched Robertson lead his team to victory in the state tournament. They were so excited they couldn't sleep.

They were also ecstatic when they spotted Robertson at a track meet at the University of Indiana. The identical twins, who would be standouts in both Indiana high school and Indiana University basketball before going on to fine professional careers in the NBA, shyly asked him for an autograph. Robertson agreed, but he was holding a hot dog in one hand and a paper in the other. He stuck the hot dog in his varsity jacket pocket and signed. Tom still had Robertson's autograph after the twins retired from basketball.

As to Robertson's basketball accomplishments, "Nothing Oscar ever did shocked me," Coach Crowe told David Benner, a reporter for the *Indianapolis Star.* "It really didn't. There were things I thought he would do because he had the ability to do it. The most outstanding things about Oscar are his all-around skills, ability, and leadership qualities.

"I think it was unique to find someone as versatile as Oscar. There were players good in this area or that area, but not many, if any, as versatile as Robertson. Plus, he was demanding of teammates. He expected from them what he was giving."

Those same qualities would characterize Robertson's approach to the game and his teammates throughout his career.

"He was really a coach's dream," according to Ridley. "Here was a guy who had honed and developed his skills so well, he was able to pass things on. When he saw that guys weren't matching up to what they should have been doing, he was always a taskmaster about it. And that's what it takes when you have that kind of God-given gift. That's why Oscar and some others stand out above the rest."

Racism Rears Its Head

Robertson, expressing admiration for his coach, commented on his Web site, "He came along at the right time [when sports were only beginning to be integrated] and handled the situation perfectly. It was the greatest time for our school because I think we helped people see they could get beyond racial issues to a common topic of discussion, which was high school basketball."

But racism was still rampant in Indiana and all over the nation. America was quickly becoming a country of wealthy consumers, but areas of the South were still stricken with poverty. All over the nation, African Americans were demanding the civil rights that they had always been denied. Robertson, who, until the Indiana-Kentucky high school all-star basketball game, had never played on a team with white players, alleged that there was some one-sided officiating and crowd hostility when he played for Attucks High. Then, when the team won its 1955 championship, city officials were uneasy about the possible nature of the victory celebration and required the players to have their party out of town.

"After we won, they drove us around in a fire truck through town and back to Northwestern Park to have a bonfire there [rather than in the city]," Robertson recalled. The reason? Robertson told the *Indianapolis Star,* "They said the blacks are gonna tear up [the city's] downtown." It was something Robertson would never forget.

But there were also positive experiences Robertson would long remember, too. Thirty-five years after graduation from Crispus Attucks High School, the superstar athlete, who was in the top 10 percent of his class there, and who always had great respect for education, told a newspaper writer, "I will never forget my caring teachers in high school in Indianapolis."

On-Court Glory,
Off-Court Racism

Robertson was heavily recruited by eager colleges as a three-time all-state athlete at Crispus Attucks High. He chose the University of Cincinnati, among other reasons because it was close enough to Indianapolis for him to visit home regularly. Another reason for his choice was that Cincinnati had a co-op program, which meant he could alternately work and attend class seven weeks at a time. While studying for his business administration degree, he reportedly earned $1.80 an hour at the Cincinnati Gas and Electricity Company. Also, he'd heard about poor racial attitudes at other nearby colleges.

Still, at the University of Cincinnati, he was the only African American on what

24

Oscar Robertson makes a jump shot during an NCAA game against Iowa University on December 1, 1959.

previously had been an all-white team. But Robertson was up for the challenge.

The most memorable game of his collegiate career, he said on his Web site, was "the first one," even though he can't recall who the opponent was. "It was memorable to me because it was a new beginning. I had had success in high school and received national attention; now I was taking my game to a new level of competition and I had to deliver. I was primed."

In the three seasons he played varsity ball for the university (1957–1958, 1958–1959, and 1959–1960), Oscar established himself as the finest basketball player ever to perform for the Cincinnati Bearcats and one of the best, if not the best, player in the history of college basketball.

He scored 2,973 points in 88 games, a record-setting per-game average of 33.8 points. And while his high scoring earned him the most attention, he excelled in other categories as well. He led the team in rebounding all three years with an average of 15.2 rebounds per game, and he dazzled fans and players with his outstanding playmaking.

In one game, Robertson set a school record of 13 assists.

By the time his college career was over, he held virtually every one of the university's major scoring and rebounding records, as well as fourteen National Collegiate Athletic Association (NCAA) records and most of the top scoring marks in the Missouri Valley Conference.

Robertson, six feet five inches, played the forward position most of the time, but he was versatile enough to go into the pivot or bring the ball up the floor as a guard. Even playing in the forward position, he still retained such guard skills as dribbling the ball. And thanks to his quick moves and feints (fake-outs), he did most of his scoring inside, but he could also be extremely accurate from the outside.

He led the Bearcats to two Final Fours and a 79–9 record during his three varsity seasons. At Madison Square Garden, as a sophomore in an NCAA tournament game, he scored a record 56 points and three times in a row won the Gold Star Memorial Award, given to the outstanding visiting college player performing at the Garden.

In February 1959, when the Bearcats were playing a weak North Texas State team, Robertson outdid himself in scoring. Missing just one shot, the Big O had 25 points at halftime alone. Then, after the intermission, his total quickly passed 30 and 40 points and, when he had 52, Coach George Smith sat him down. But the crowd screamed for more, and with his teammates feeding him again and again, he ended with 62 points, both a university and Missouri Valley Conference record.

His accomplishments did not go unnoticed.

Three times a unanimous all-American, Robertson was the first player to lead the nation in scoring for three straight seasons with 35.1 points per game in 1957–1958, 32.6 per game in 1958–1959, and 33.7 in 1959–1960. He ended as the NCAA's all-time scoring leader at the time. His 2,973 points later made him the seventh all-time scorer in NCAA history.

He was also the first player to be named Player of the Year three times by United Press International and *The Sporting News*. For two straight years, he led the balloting for the

Associated Press all-American team, and for two years in succession was named College Player of the Year by the U.S. Basketball Writers. Because of his accomplishments, the College Player of the Year award was renamed The Oscar Robertson Trophy by the Basketball Writers, beginning with the 1968 Men's Final Four.

Oscar cocaptained the Bearcats in his junior and senior seasons, and led the team to the Final Four twice, both in 1959 and 1960. The Bearcats were expected to win the national championship those years but lost in the semifinals each time.

Oscar's brilliance carried over into several postseason all-star contests. Twice named to play in the East-West Shrine Game, he was its leading scorer and Most Outstanding Player in 1959 at Kansas City, and the leading scorer in the Pan-American Games that summer.

Life Wasn't Always Glorious

Despite his magnificent on-court accomplishments, life was far from perfect for Robertson.

GOLD STAR AWARD
OUTSTANDING VISITING
1959 - 60
THIRD CONSECUTIVE SE
OSCAR ROBERTS
UNIVERSITY OF CINCI
PRESENTED BY
METROPOLITAN BASKETBALL WR

In spite of being the only African American on what previously had been an all-white team, he said he had never thought in terms of playing against whites or blacks. "I had never in my life thought about color until somebody mentioned it to me," he recalled in an article written by Paul Hemphill. Many of those mentions were offensive—curses and racial taunts—and there were some very racist practices.

For instance, he decided one time to stay away from a Cincinnati pool hall when he realized he was the only black allowed in and only because he was a basketball star.

Worse, in North Carolina, the Ku Klux Klan, a hate group that has terrorized African Americans since 1866, sent Robertson a death threat. Robertson had to contend not only with racial slurs but also a black cat placed in his locker. Topping off the meanness, the Bearcats weren't allowed to stay in a hotel because of the presence of an African American (Robertson) on the team.

More racism followed. When the Bearcats came to Houston, Texas, for a game, Oscar

Oscar Robertson shows off the Gold Star award he won in 1960 for being judged the most outstanding visiting college player at New York City's Madison Square Garden.

wasn't allowed to stay at the all-white hotel where his teammates stayed, and instead he had to sleep in a dorm at a black university fourteen miles away.

"I was lying on my bunk out there at Texas Southern, wondering why it had to be me," he remembered. "I thought, 'This is the last time I want to hear anything about team unity. The college uses you, and then this happens,'" he told Hemphill.

The only reason he didn't quit, he said, was he knew the coach (George Smith) had nothing to do with it, and from then on, the team was never booked into a hotel that wouldn't accommodate Robertson.

Recalling the racial insults and insensitivity he encountered, Robertson told the *Indianapolis Star,* "I'll never forgive them. But that's the way it was then, so you had to make the adjustment. I think I made the adjustment, but now I don't have to anymore."

And, thanks in great measure to Robertson's trailblazing, when Cincinnati won the NCAA Championship the year after his graduation, four starters on the team were African Americans.

Big "O"—As in Olympics

It followed that after graduation Oscar was able to try out for the United States Olympic team in 1960. Rising to the occasion as he always did, Robertson was a tournament high scorer as he led a college all-star team to victory in the Olympic Trials in Denver, Colorado.

Accordingly, Oscar was a unanimous selection for the U.S. Olympic team that would compete later that summer in the seventeenth Olympiad, in Rome, Italy. Not only was the Big O a unanimous choice, but he was given the added honor of being named the team's cocaptain with another future NBA superstar, Jerry West.

"The Olympics were significant," Robertson told fans on his Web site, "because you had to make the team, and then you had the honor of representing your country against the best athletes from all over the world." He later told the Denver Post, "The Olympics would rank

Jerry West *(second from left)* and Oscar Robertson accept congratulations
from basketball players representing the Soviet Union *(left)* and Brazil *(right)*
at the Olympics in Rome, Italy, in 1960.

ahead of anything else for me. It's something you
dream about all your life. It was tremendous for
me to be in the Olympic Village along with
thousands of athletes from everywhere."

In 1960, the United States Olympic team
was described as the greatest in history, and
possibly the greatest group of amateur
basketball talent ever assembled. (It wasn't until
later Olympiads that professional basketball
players were permitted to play.) According to

USA Basketball, the 1960 team was so perfectly balanced that no one player emerged as a dominant star. Ten of the twelve players on the U.S. roster went on to play in the NBA.

The U.S. squad swept eight games, led by Robertson and West, each of whom scored 136 points, an average of 17 a game. Three other U.S. players also averaged in double figures for the eight contests. The Americans took the first game, 88–54, against host team Italy, with Robertson and Adrian Smith each scoring 16 points. They then walloped Japan, 125–66, and Hungary, 107–63.

In the semifinal round, the Americans opened up a 32–1 lead and whipped Yugoslavia, 104–42. Against the next opponent, Uruguay, the U.S. team racked up its fourth straight 100-plus-point game, winning 108–50.

A contest against the Soviet Union would close out the semifinals. The Soviets had a formidable lineup, led by Jan Kruminsh, who was seven feet three inches tall and weighed 320 pounds. But the U.S. team, after leading at halftime 35–28, opened the second half with 20 points in the first five minutes, putting the game out of reach. Paced by West, the U.S. team won with a score of 81–57.

In the final round, the U.S. routed Italy, 112–81, with six players in double figures, led by Jerry Lucas's 25. Lucas repeated the 25-point total in the final against Brazil, a 90–63 victory for the Americans—and the cherished gold medal for everyone on the team.

The U.S. Olympic winning streak now totaled 36 games with an average of 101.9 points and a margin of victory of 42.4 points a game!

Robertson, who contributed 51 field goals and 34 free throws on 50 attempts, considered his Olympic gold medal win second in career highlights only to his amazing athletic achievements in high school.

An Imposing Figure

Robertson's accomplishments as an amateur basketball player echoed for years afterward.

In October 1994, the University of Cincinnati, which had retired his number 12 at the end of the 1959–1960 season, unveiled an

Basketball coach George Smith presents Oscar Robertson with a number 12 jersey during a ceremony retiring the athlete's number at the University of Cincinnati Field House on March 28, 1960.

eight-foot statue of Robertson in recognition of his contributions to the university. Cincinnati alumnus J.W. Brown donated the money for the statue, which was sculpted by Blair Buswell.

At the unveiling of the statue, Robertson's voice trembled as he recalled the racial indignities he had had to suffer. "This statue is for Oscar Robertson," he told the overflow crowd, "but it's also for you."

In an article by Bill Koch of the *Cincinnati Post*, Robertson explained that the emotion he displayed was not about his play or what had happened to him in some of those incidents. "The emotion was about some of the people I knew at the university and whether or not some of those people could have averted some of those incidents. That's what the emotion was about."

He added, "You have highs and lows in life. I always say in order to write love songs, you have to have some bad times. If that's the case I could write the greatest love songs in the world."

"I was just a young man who wanted to win, [who] loved playing basketball, and who wanted to get an education."

NBA Sensation

There was no question that Robertson was headed for a professional basketball career, and a great one. Drafted by the Cincinnati Royals of the NBA, Robertson, who as a child was too poor to own a basketball, signed a contract for $33,000 a year, and would later earn considerably more.

While African Americans would eventually dominate the NBA, there were not many in the league in its infancy. Robertson remarked in a fiftieth-anniversary interview for the NBA, "A lot of blacks who were great players didn't make the teams because they didn't want too many on the team."

He believed that in the early 1960s, when African Americans were beginning to star in the

NBA, there was a quota system. "We never had more than three blacks on our team and when we traveled they always made sure we stayed together. I can't imagine people being that narrow-minded," he was quoted in a 1981 article that appeared in the *St. Louis Globe-Democrat.*

There were just eight teams when Robertson entered the league and, in his words, "It was such a tremendous competition." The rivalry brought out the best in him, and he was an immediate sensation. In his rookie season (1960–1961), Oscar finished third in the league in scoring, with an average of 30.5 points a game, and was voted NBA Rookie of the Year.

As expected, he was also elected to play for the Western Division in the NBA's all-star game. Not only did he play, but he won the game's Most Valuable Player (MVP) award after scoring 23 points and setting an assists record with 14, one better than the previous mark set by Bob Cousy.

It wasn't the last time he'd break a Cousy record. For eight straight years in regular season play, Cousy had led the league in assists,

Oscar Robertson wins the MVP award at the Holiday Festival at Madison Square Garden on December 30, 1960.

but that season Robertson ended Cousy's eight-year streak with 9.7 assists per game.

In regular season play, the last-place Cincinnati team still had problems. Although Robertson's teammate Jack Twyman tossed in 25.3 points a game, the lowly Royals improved only to a record of 33–46 and were still stuck in the division cellar.

Triple-Double—for a Season!

In his next season, Robertson's talents truly blossomed. A statistical mark of a great game is known as a triple-double, meaning that a player has garnered double figures, ten or more, in at least three categories, usually points, rebounds, and assists. In only his second year in the NBA, (1961–1962), Robertson did something no one else had ever accomplished: He averaged a triple-double for the entire season!

That season, he averaged 30.8 points, 12.5 rebounds, and 11.4 assists per game, and the next season, he came close to repeating the remarkable feat, averaging 28.3 points, 10.4 rebounds, and 9.5 assists a game. In fact, he averaged a triple-double over his first five NBA seasons.

Interviewed by NBA Entertainment, Inc., about the likelihood of anyone matching his triple-double full-season feat, Robertson said, "Records are made to be broken. But I don't anticipate anyone in the foreseeable future doing it—maybe in the year 2020. I don't think the players now have put in enough time on the court to get that accomplished. Many triple-doubles are players who get 10 points a game, with 10 or 11 rebounds, but when I did it, I averaged over 30 points a game."

He continued, "We weren't totally aware" of setting records at the time. "We were just out there playing basketball. It was something that we had done all of our lives, and just to extend it on into the pro ranks was tremendous for us. It was a dream come true."

Another dream that came true for the Big O was competing against the greatest athletes in basketball. "The collection of guys who came along at that time . . . who really formed the history of basketball . . . is tremendous . . . No money in the world is worth it for me not to have played during those times," he added in the same interview.

Whoever his opponent might be, even someone of the gigantic stature and talent of a Wilt Chamberlain or Bill Russell, Robertson remained in control. He never showed any specific emotion to his teammates, especially if he was nervous or rattled.

Robertson remembered that his high school coach had told him he was expected to do certain things for the team as a point guard. He kept them within himself and never revealed his true feelings to the other players.

"It's the way I was, the way my demeanor is. I don't get upset very easily about anything. You can't get upset in a game because a lot of people push you, elbow you, do certain things, call you names [trying to] get you upset to throw you off from the . . . duties you have to do," he explained to NBA Entertainment.

With his 899 assists that 1961–1962 season, Robertson was again league champion in that

Basketball: From Drudgery to Art

Robertson titled a book he wrote with Michael O'Daniel in the late 1990s *The Art of Basketball*. He chose that title, he wrote in the introduction, "because I believe basketball *is* an art. When the game is played as it should be played, you'll see athletes perform with precision, finesse, rhythm, flair, and grace."

Robertson said he learned how to play the game by playing fundamentals first—"rebounding, positioning, defense, passing—all those things that really are drudgery on the court."

He feels the modern game is somewhat lacking in these fundamentals. "Look at high school games," he said. "You get a little pressure and people fall apart. Look at college games. People get a little pressure, they don't know what to do with the ball. They see a simple zone and they don't know where to go. There's something wrong."

Writer Bill Koch said of Robertson, "He was a great player because of his devotion to basics. He didn't try to dribble through three defenders when he could pass to an open man. He understood the flow of the game. He used his head as much as his physical skills."

department, breaking another record by Cousy, who had 715 assists two years earlier.

More important than personal accomplishments, Robertson led the Royals to the first of six consecutive trips to the playoffs, but that season they were eliminated in the first round by the Detroit Pistons.

As the team's "field general," he felt responsible for how his team fared. He said others expected he could come in and win every game.

While he thought that might have been possible if he had shot the ball every time, neither his teammates nor management would have liked one player taking so many shots. It would have meant the Royals lacked a team concept. Still, he felt that the Royals wanted him to act more as a team player than as a star shooter, even though a few critics contended that he could sometimes be a "ball hog," a charge others strongly denied.

Teammate Jerry Lucas, who joined the Royals in the 1963–1964 season, commented, "If Oscar really sets out to see how many points he can score in a single game, there's no telling how high he can go."

Yet Robertson has insisted that he didn't go out in the game to shoot initially. His goal was to run the offense and act as one component of the whole team—no matter its ability.

"You're only going to win as a team. Sure, you must have stars on your team in order to win . . . Somebody has to put the ball in the basket. But still it's a team game, and as a point guard, I wanted to get other guys involved in the offense. That was my chore," he said in an interview for NBA Entertainment.

Always an All-Star

Robertson would be named to the all-star squad in twelve of the fourteen seasons he played in the NBA, virtually all of them on the winning side. In three years (1961, 1964, and 1969), the Big O was named MVP of those contests that featured the league's top players.

Robertson played for the Western Division all-stars his first two seasons and, with him leading the way, the West scored 153

and 150 points, respectively, the largest totals ever in an all-star game. When expansion caused a realignment of teams, Cincinnati shifted to the Eastern Division, and Oscar played on the its squad, which he led to four consecutive victories.

Improving, but Still a Ways to Go

In the 1962–1963 season, the Royals got past the Syracuse Nationals in the division semifinals and, with Robertson in top form, in the next round forced the Boston Celtics to a seventh and deciding game. But the decision went to the Celtics, who would go on to win the NBA championship.

In the 1963–1964 season, Robertson was so outstanding, he not only was selected as the MVP in the all-star game, his second such honor, but was also named the league's MVP for the entire regular season. It was a tremendous tribute.

"He is so great he scares me," Red Auerbach, then the Boston Celtics' head coach,

Oscar Robertson receives the MVP trophy for his outstanding 1963–1964 season performance.

said about Robertson, who that season led the league in assists (11 a game) and free-throw percentage (.853), and who was second in scoring (31.4 points a game) only to Wilt Chamberlain.

Auerbach once joked that he told his players to stretch out their fingers extra wide while guarding the Big O but that Robertson shot the ball through their fingers anyway.

Jerry Lucas added, "He obviously was unbelievable and way ahead of his time. There is no more complete player than Robertson." The late great Wilt Chamberlain agreed in an article by Carl Martin in the *City Dispatch*, "Oscar Robertson is not as fast as some or as good a shot as others, but he knows how to put everything together better than anybody else."

Ever the perfectionist, Robertson never stopped practicing and never stopped trying to improve his skills. You could say he was definitely a "money player," a competitor who was at his best when the chips were down. Once, when the new Royals coach, Jack McMahon, offered five dollars to the player who could sink the most free throws in practice, Oscar hit 25 of 25!

Robertson, who thrived on pressure, thought that the stress and anxiety he felt improved his game. He felt that no other person—player or coach—could stop him from meeting his goals.

Throughout the 1960s, Robertson continuously maintained a high per-game average of points, assists, and rebounds.

Late in the 1967–1968 season, Tom Van Arsdale was traded by the Detroit Pistons to the Royals, then coached by Ed Jucker. Van Arsdale had mixed emotions about the trade, but he was delighted he'd be a teammate of his longtime hero, the Big O.

"I don't know whether he realizes it," Van Arsdale recalled in *Our Basketball Lives*, his autobiography with his brother Dick, "but he probably did more to put confidence in me as to what I could do in professional basketball than anyone else. Here, I'd just come off the bench in Detroit and naturally a little shy about shooting a lot, but Robertson would say, 'If you've got the open shot, take it. If you miss, just keep shooting and don't worry about it.'

Oscar Robertson dribbles past Sam Jones during a game against the Celtics at the Boston Garden on April 10, 1963.

"And then I'd watch him and see how much confidence he had—knowing he could do anything he wanted to do, and then I'd ask myself why I'm not like that. I really changed my attitude. I'd go out there and if I did something wrong, I'd say 'the heck with it' and just keep on going."

Oscar's helpfulness and encouragement didn't prevent him from being critical when it was merited. "Oh, he's very critical of his teammates if they do anything wrong," Van Arsdale wrote. "Not that it's anything personal. It's just that he wants to win. He's so good at what he does; if he sees somebody do it the wrong way, he's got to say something. He can't understand why somebody can make a mistake on something that seems so easy to him. Robertson is a very intelligent guy, and he's most upset when somebody makes a mental mistake."

Sometimes it was an official who, in Robertson's opinion, had made a mental mistake, and he would let him know about it.

According to Tom Callihan of *Time* magazine, Robertson "was an angry guy, and he had reason to be. It affected his game. I think he played his absolute best when he was furious."

As to charges that he screamed at players, Robertson explained that—although it was rare—he sometimes had to be vocal to get the team's plays across because of the yelling in the stands.

There were other reasons for his exasperation. As Robertson explained in an interview for NBA Entertainment, "You're playing with a team struggling to make .500 or just get in the playoffs and you throw a ball to a guy and he misses a wide-open layup, you're upset, because you may not get that chance again. On a team with all-Americans, [who] can rebound and come back, maybe you don't say that much. Star players had to have confidence in people they were playing with. If they don't, you're frustrated—very frustrated."

Van Arsdale felt privileged to be on the receiving end of Robertson's 6,950th assist, breaking another Cousy record at the time. The pass was described as "swift enough to give Van Arsdale time, soft enough to handle, and chest-high for the ultimate in shooting convenience."

Afterward, Van Arsdale commented, "Everything is basic with Robertson. He takes advantage of every little wrong move by the opposition. He throws passes I would never dream of throwing. He has supreme confidence. He can do anything, anytime.

"If you're open, you just know you'll get the ball. The main thing in playing with Robertson is just to keep moving and never turn your head. He instills confidence in other players because he's so sure of himself. We all feel that if we can just stay close in a game, Robertson will win it."

"I knew the game. I felt the game," Robertson told Mike Bass in the *Cincinnati Post*. "I don't think there was anyone as good at getting the ball to the right person at the right time as I was . . . With a minute or thirty seconds left, you don't want to pass to a guy who can't shoot free throws or take the ball to the basket."

He emphasized the same point to sports writer Carl Martin, "All passes aren't good passes just because the ball reaches the teammate you intend it for. Playmaking is getting the ball so that he is in a position to take his best shot."

Robertson would end his career with a total of 9,887 assists (an NBA record until it was broken by Magic Johnson, who said he learned his skills by copying Robertson).

Robertson insists that if statisticians gave assists then as they do now, he'd have had "another six or seven thousand." In a 1991 interview with the *Cincinnati Post,* he pointed out that in the 1960s and 1970s, "you had to earn an assist"—a player had to pass the ball to a teammate who scored right off the pass, without dribbling. "Now if you throw to a guy at half-court and he dribbles down court and shoots a twenty-footer and scores, that's an assist."

Robertson said in the *Washington Post,* "I wish someone would go back and look at a play-by-play of one of my games and record assists the way they do today. I'd probably have 25 a game."

Oscar Robertson poses with Boston Celtics star Bob Cousy before a game at the Boston Garden on November 5, 1960.

The Coming of Bob Cousy

Season after season, Robertson had led the Royals to the playoffs, only to be eliminated, usually in an early round. Then, Cincinnati missed the playoffs two years in a row and attendance dwindled. Trying to turn things around, the Royals hired Bob Cousy, the electrifying basketball great who had sparked the Boston Celtics for thirteen seasons, to replace Ed Jucker as coach for the 1969–1970 season.

Cousy stressed a running attack, with emphasis on the fast-break, and a pressure defense. Robertson, who'd been accustomed to taking most of the team's shots, was told to pass off more, to give the team a more balanced offense. At first Robertson was passing the ball too much, and the change in play was beginning to affect the team's scoring abilities.

To draw fans and generate some excitement, Cousy, then forty-one years old, even put on a uniform and played seven games in the back court with Robertson. In one of those games, Cousy had five fouls charged against him during his seven minutes of game time.

Some observers contended that Robertson's style of completely controlling the game didn't fit into the running-game style of play Cousy was trying to establish, and that his new system, with its emphasis on youth, either left Robertson out of the offense, or used him as a decoy.

Still, Robertson felt he'd been playing pretty well. "Bob's system," he said in an article in the *Cincinnati Enquirer*, "is a change for me, and I've got to adjust to it. That's up to me; that's my job. Bob's entitled to coach the team any way he wants."

But it was a less-than-happy mixture. Some noted that Robertson's best playing years were behind him, others that playing ten years without a championship had drained him of motivation. Also, there appeared to be a quiet sort of personality clash between Robertson and Cousy, and there were those who even speculated that Cousy had never forgiven Robertson for breaking so many of his own records. In any event, Robertson's days with the team appeared to be numbered.

Nevertheless, it was a major jolt to Cincinnati fans to hear on April 21, 1970, that the Big O had been traded from Cincinnati to Milwaukee for Flynn Robinson and Charlie Paulk.

"Whatever Cousy's reasons for trading me might have been," Robertson later told the *Cincinnati Post*, "I think he was wrong and I'll never forget it."

Robertson had originally been slated to move to Baltimore and was bothered that he hadn't been consulted on that projected trade. But when he learned of it, he exercised the clause in his contract that gave him the right to approve which team could have him. Turning down a trade to the Baltimore Bullets, he chose the Milwaukee Bucks instead.

Traded Up

With all of his magnificent accomplishments, one goal had eluded Robertson: a championship. He, like all professional basketball players, yearned for a championship ring.

Now with the Milwaukee Bucks, there was renewed hope, although when he joined them, the Bucks were struggling. But, thanks in great measure to Robertson's versatility, experience, and intensity, the team, coached by former NBA guard Larry Costello, began to realize its potential.

Though thirty-one years old and past his prime, Robertson sparked his new teammates, among them second-year player Kareem Abdul-Jabbar (then known as Lew Alcindor), who

would become a premier, dominating force in professional basketball.

"When Oscar came, he made it impossible for teams to defend us," commented Jabbar, who observers knew would be better with a knowledgeable passer in the lineup. "When you had [Oscar] to run the plays, anything you drew up would work."

Ray Patterson, the team's president, commented in the *Cincinnati Post*, "When we got Robertson, we were a new franchise."

And Robertson, not one for false modesty, agreed. He knew that the team was headed in a new direction with him on board.

Under his leadership, they were.

"When I first got to Milwaukee, Kareem was not the player that he was going to be," Robertson told NBA Entertainment. "He learned a lot of basketball when we were playing on the Bucks. I thought he was the greatest shot off the pivot I'd ever seen in the history of the game."

Inspired by the Big O, the player one writer called "the cool quarterback" of the Milwaukee offensive, the team rolled through its

Oscar Robertson's ability to evade defenders and advance the basketball up the court made it easier for his Milwaukee Bucks teammates to score.

opponents. By November 1970, the Bucks picked up their seventh victory in a row, with a win over the Boston Celtics. When his team trailed by 10 points Robertson took charge, leading Milwaukee to a victory. He scored 26 points, with 9 rebounds and 10 assists, but the statistics told only a part of the story.

"It was a great basketball game," said Bucks coach Larry Costello, "and the guy who brought us back was Oscar. When things were going bad for us in the third quarter, he put everything back together. He made the shots. He made the passes. He got the rebounds. He just did a heck of a job."

John Havlicek of the Celtics, an outstanding player himself, agreed. "Oscar's in charge. He stands out there with the ball and waits until [Jabbar] and the corner men make their cuts and then he hits the open man. The Bucks were tough enough to defend against before Robertson got there. Now they're just about impossible."

And so it went, as the Bucks swept through their division. In a game against the New York Knicks in January 1971, Robertson was forced into his old control style of play because Jabbar ran into foul trouble and was on the bench for nearly half of the game. The Bucks won, 116–106, giving them a 33–7 record.

"I didn't feel any particular pressure," Robertson, who scored a season high of 35 points while contributing 13 assists and 9 rebounds, told Bob Wolf of the *Milwaukee Journal*. "It was just another game to me. When Kareem went out, I had to play more like I did at Cincinnati . . . My best game? I don't know. Points mean a lot, but they don't mean everything."

Coach Costello felt that Robertson had played his best game of the year. "He was fantastic. That's the way I wish he'd play all the time."

Knicks center Willis Reed agreed, "Robertson did it all. That's his game; he runs the team. Many people say he's fat and out of shape, but he doesn't play like it. We could have come back, but he wouldn't let it happen."

The Bucks, in only their third year as an NBA franchise, kept rolling along. As the regular season neared its close in March 1971,

the Bucks registered their nineteenth victory in a row, defeating the Detroit Pistons, 108–95, with Robertson contributing 16 assists. Milwaukee ended the season on top of the Midwest Division with a 66–16 record (improved from 56–26 and a second-place division finish a year earlier, pre-Robertson).

In the 1970–1971 playoffs, the Bucks' momentum continued. With teammate Lucius Allen out of action, Robertson had to get out his artillery. Perhaps he was searching for his shots more carefully. Whether or not that was the reason, Milwaukee lost only a single game in each playoff series against San Francisco and Los Angeles, and was more than ready to meet the Baltimore Bullets in the NBA Finals.

The Meaning of Basketball

To Robertson, basketball is "a tremendous game. It teaches you a lot of things about life . . . about different people.

"Before, it was a way of life. A time, an era that Americans really needed in order to go forward to be influenced by certain

Oscar Robertson jumps to make a basket against the New York Knicks in March 1974.

individuals, to help them, to give people goals to shoot for, or aspirations," Robertson told NBA Entertainment.

"A kid would see Hector Camacho boxing and say, 'I want to be like Camacho.' See Joe Louis or Sugar Ray, 'I want to be like Sugar Ray.'

"It was a way out of a desperate situation. That's what sports were, especially basketball. That's what it meant to me, because it was a way of life. It was a social thing to go and play sports because you had nothing else to do, rather than steal and get into trouble."

At Long Last, a Championship

Oscar Robertson closed his eyes and let out a yell of delight. "Whoo-ee," he shouted. "Whoo-ee." He was jumping up and down like a child whose dream had just come true.

The scene was the visitors' locker room at the Civic Center in Baltimore on April 30, 1971, and his Bucks had just disarmed the Bullets, 118–106, to sweep the NBA Finals and win the NBA championship that Robertson had eagerly awaited for more than a decade. The Bucks had taken the first three games by scores of 98–88, 102–83, and 107–99.

In the fourth and final contest, the Big O scored 30 points and had 9 assists, although

Baltimore coach Gene Shue had tried five different players to defend against him, to no avail. As Jack Kiser of the *Philadelphia News* described it, "He beat them all with ease, shooting over the men who were shorter, and driving around the men who were taller."

"He was perfect," declared Milwaukee coach Costello, noting that Jabbar "is our arms and legs, but Robertson is our brains, our eyes, and our heart." While not yet the dominant player he would become, Jabbar led the league in scoring that season with an average of 31.7 points per game, and otherwise excelled so much that he was voted the NBA's Most Valuable Player. But, in his opinion, it was Robertson who deserved the MVP award.

"Everybody did his job," Jabbar said of each of his teammates. "But the man who did it most is sitting over there. Oscar gets my vote for MVP. He made it easy."

In the physical game, Jack Kiser of the *Philadelphia News* wrote, "there was Robertson, telling everybody to simmer down and play basketball . . . directing every movement of the team chewing his man up on offense and holding [Earl "the Pearl"] Monroe to 12 points on defense."

"They said I never won anything," Robertson told reporters. "Now they can't say that anymore . . . I honestly can't tell you how happy that makes me feel.

"How happy? [I was] so happy I can't explain it. Much happier than I thought I would ever be. I knew we would beat Baltimore and I was going to play it cool, not get excited. But there's something about winning a championship that makes you lose your cool," he recalled for NBA Entertainment.

On the court, Robertson kept his cool, keeping the Bucks from shooting until the shot was there. Losing coach Shue had nothing but praise for Robertson. "He was the leader. He hit the open man and he played tremendous defense. I said when they got him, they would be the best team in basketball."

Everyone agreed. The Big O could do it all. "There is nothing he can't do," former

Boston Celtics coach and general manager Red Auerbach said of Robertson. "No one comes close to him or has the ability to break open a game like Oscar . . . He can beat you all by himself and usually does."

As celebrated as the Big O was for his offense, his defensive skills were equally remarkable, especially as evidenced in the NBA Finals that year.

According to Costello, Robertson (a future member of the Wisconsin Sports Hall of Fame) helped the Bucks on defense as much as he did on offense throughout the season. "He plays even better defense than Walt Frazier of the New York Knicks. He's stronger than Frazier, and nobody is going to take him inside and get six-foot shots . . . If anybody scores against Robertson, they're going to have to do it on 18-footers."

Coach Shue wholeheartedly agreed. "Robertson should have been on the all-defensive team. He got my vote. He may have played better defense than any other guard in the league this year. When a man is a great

Oscar Robertson dribbles by a defender during a game.

offensive player and he's as smart as Oscar is, he knows what the other offensive player is going to do, and that helps him tremendously on defense."

"The proof of Robertson's virtuosity," according to a *Los Angeles Times* writer, "is that, in his waning years, overweight, and over aged, and plagued with the slow-healing infirmities these conditions produce, Robertson was [still] able to steer a team to a world championship."

The Robertson Rule

Oscar Robertson also helped steer NBA players to better conditions.

From 1963 to 1974, he was president of the NBA Players Association, and when the NBA planned to merge with the old American Basketball Association (ABA), the players' union objected. They argued that such a merger would seriously hamper competition in the signing of players and if a player didn't want to play with a certain team, he could be blackballed forever.

In support of these feelings, the Players Association filed an antitrust lawsuit, which took the name of the association president, Oscar Robertson. It challenged not only the proposed merger, but also the legality of the college draft and the NBA's reserve clause, which prohibited players from becoming free agents and signing with any team they chose. Under the reserve clause, a player might have to stay with one team for his entire career.

It took six years for the suit to be settled, but in 1976 (two years after Robertson's retirement), it was agreed that the leagues could merge and the draft could remain intact. Drafted players, however, now had the right to say no to a team that wanted them for a year and could reenter the draft. Also, when a team signed a free-agent player, it didn't have to compensate the other team, so this encouraged the signing of more free agents and eventually led to higher salaries for all professional players.

Even though Robertson had retired by the time the suit settled and become president of the

Retired NBA Players Association, the agreement is known to this day as the Robertson Rule.

All Good Things Must End

Although his legs were starting to weaken and he considered retiring, Robertson and the other Bucks hoped to repeat their championship. But in the 1971–1972 season, after finishing first in the Midwest Division and beating the Golden State Warriors in the conference semifinals, they lost the Western Conference finals in six games to the Los Angeles Lakers, the eventual champions.

In the next season (1972–1973), they finished first in their division again, but they lost to Golden State in the conference semifinals.

The Big O still demonstrated flashes of brilliance. The game in which the Bucks clinched the Midwest Division championship for the third straight time made Ray Scott, the coach of their opponents, the Detroit Pistons, comment, "Oscar should get an Oscar for his performance. I haven't seen him play like that in years."

One headlong, floor-length dash to the basket caused Robertson's own coach, Costello, to leap from the bench and yell, "Way to go, Oscar." After the game, he added, "Oscar was just fantastic. He looked like he was twenty years old when he went down the floor that time. He really motored—the way he used to do it all the time. When he was a kid, he maintained that speed for forty-eight minutes."

Teammate Lucius Allen commented, "When the Big O goes down court like he did tonight, I love it, I [just] love it."

In the 1973–1974 season, the Bucks came very close to another title. Again, Robertson often was a reflection of his former self, as in the game in which the Bucks defeated the Capital Bullets for their twelfth straight victory. Commenting on Robertson's 24-point performance, Bullets coach K.C. Jones, who, as a member of the Boston Celtics, had played against Robertson, said, "He's still Oscar Robertson. He still does it all. Nobody in the world can stop him when he's ready to put the ball up. He pulled his whole game out of the bag tonight."

But a month later, Robertson's ailments returned with a vengeance and he missed eleven games before returning as a part-timer. He didn't move with the ease that once characterized his game and, down the stretch of at least one important contest, he sat out the last nine minutes because the coach felt he wasn't fast enough. "It was a coach's decision and that's what he made," said Robertson, who seemed hurt by the decision, according to a *Milwaukee Journal* article by Bob Wolf.

He acknowledged that he had come back too soon. "My back was hurting, so I had to walk differently and even shoot differently. I couldn't stand up on my toes to shoot the way I've always shot. After doing it a certain way for so many years, I [just] couldn't adjust."

When he was in pain, he said, he tried only to get the ball to a teammate, not force shots. Still, some people were disappointed that he was shooting less than he normally would.

Once Robertson's back healed, he and the Bucks picked up the pace. They topped their division again, whipped the Lakers in five games in the conference semifinals, and swept the Chicago Bulls in the conference finals in four straight games.

In the Finals, they were pitted against the mighty Boston Celtics but were favored to win. Boston took the first game in Milwaukee before the Bucks tied the series in overtime. At Boston, the Celtics won the third contest, but in the fourth game the Bucks came back to even things up at two games apiece. The seesaw continued as Boston won the next at Milwaukee, only to have the Bucks tie the series for a third time, winning in double overtime on a skyhook by Jabbar in the closing seconds. But a championship for the Bucks was not to be, as Dave Cowens led Boston to a 15-point victory in the seventh and deciding game.

Just before the end of the regular season, the Bucks hosted a ceremony in Robertson's honor, which included, among others, Bill Cosby, the Reverend Jesse Jackson, and Patrick J. Lucy, the governor of Wisconsin.

Some thought Robertson would use the occasion to announce his retirement. But that

81

Because his was a presence that was so respected on the court, Robertson's autograph was one of the most sought-after signatures in the 1960s and 1970s.

didn't happen until after the playoffs. And when it did, his presence was sorely missed.

A Magnificent Career

Again and again, basketball observers emphasized that the Big O could do it all. According to the *NBA at 50*, which highlights fifty years of the league's history, "He was an unstoppable offensive player, who could score from every spot on the court, and in any manner he saw fit. His offensive prowess changed the point guard stereotype from simply a passer and floor general to a scorer and offensive weapon."

He was a marvelous defensive asset, too. As Tom Callihan of *Time* magazine wrote, "Oscar Robertson . . . turned the ball over about once a month. He was the most efficient player."

On offense, Callihan wrote, "The game was geometry to him. If you gave him an 18-footer, he wanted a 15-footer. He was constantly getting closer to the basket. He seemed to want the foul as much as the shot. Robertson saw things in the game players don't see now, or very few do."

In his fourteen years as a professional player Robertson was unstoppable, but he was often critical of the game itself. In later years he declared that the players lacked dedication and strategy. He claimed that both players and their fans wanted to achieve instant success. He didn't think players wanted to work for years earning their titles and breaking records. "Everything has changed because of the nature of the game itself. People want instant dunking success. They don't want to work for it," he was quoted in a *Time* article.

Robertson's record-breaking success was hard to beat. In 1,040 games, he scored 26,710 points (an average of 25.7 per game), 9,887 assists (9.5 per game), and 7,804 rebounds (7.5 per game). At the time of his retirement, he was the NBA's all-time leader in career assists (a distinction he would hold for seventeen years), the leader in free throws made (7,694), and the league's top-scoring guard. He led the league in assists six times and in free-throw percentage twice, and his teams made the playoffs in ten of his fourteen years in the league.

In 86 postseason games, he averaged 22.2 points, 8.9 assists, and 6.7 rebounds.

A significant addition to the many honors he had already received came in 1979 when Robertson was elected to the Naismith Memorial Basketball Hall of Fame. And when all-time teams were chosen in conjunction with the NBA's thirty-fifth and then its fiftieth anniversary, Robertson was a natural selection both times.

A Higher Level

When asked to name his all-time all-star team, Robertson placed himself and Jerry West at guards, Elgin Baylor and Bob Pettit at forwards, and both Bill Russell and Wilt Chamberlain at center. He said in 1980 that he'd have to wait a few more years to see how Kareem Abdul-Jabbar developed. Robertson was hard-pressed to name the best player he ever competed against, but finally cited Baylor as the top all-around performer.

When a fan asked whether, if Robertson were a young player, he could guard Michael Jordan, the Big O replied, "I don't know if Michael Jordan could guard me. I could guard anybody, it didn't matter who it was."

And summing up his abilities, Robertson said, "I don't think I had a peer when I played basketball—in many different categories."

Many agreed with this evaluation. Bob Collins, for one, writing in the *Indianapolis Star* in 1990 about the establishment of an Oscar Robertson display at the Indiana Basketball Hall of Fame, said, "Robertson didn't play the

Oscar Robertson defends the basket against Wilt Chamberlain during a game between the Royals and the Warriors in February 1962.

game, he controlled it. His moves were subtle, the results explosive. He could put it up from outside or go to the hole. He could take off at one end and put it in at the other. And his passes were things of beauty: over the river, through the trees, and into the hands of the open man. Robertson lifted the game to a higher level."

"Am I the greatest?" Robertson asked, in response to a question. "I think I could have played against anybody; played very well against anybody.

"No one's going to ever know who's the greatest basketball player. I think I'm the greatest 'cause look at my record. They look at a guy who dunks the ball and they think that's great, but (they) can't make a free-throw, or a play, or set up on offense . . . don't know when to slow the ball down or speed it up, don't know the intangible things about basketball.

"I played as well as I could. I tried to conduct myself the way I was taught, by my coaches, my parents. That's all you can give and let the cards fall where they may."

Life After Basketball

Although Robertson was no longer an active basketball player, he still had ties to the sport after he retired from the NBA. He was briefly a commentator for ABC Radio and TV Networks and CBS-TV for NBA games. For a period, he worked with high school students in and around Cincinnati, taking them on tour a week at a time. In the fall of 1998, he took a team of retired NBA players to China for an exhibition tour against the Chinese national team.

But what occupied Robertson's attention most were his interests outside of basketball. And, in these areas, he was very successful both

Larry Bird *(left)*, Oscar Robertson, and John Wooden *(right)* meet at center court during a halftime ceremony celebrating the "50 Greatest Players in Indiana Basketball History," hosted by the Indiana Pacers on November 6, 1999.

as a businessman and a supporter of a whole host of worthy organizations and causes.

Crediting his family's Southern Baptist faith and their emphasis on education, he became very successful. In the early 1980s, Robertson, who had invested in real estate while playing for the Royals, founded Orchem, Inc., a specialty industrial chemical cleaning supplies company. He also was a principal in a trucking business and a manufacturing facility.

To improve the living conditions of African Americans in Indianapolis, Robertson helped build affordable housing. And, calling things as he saw them, he kept up his criticism of social policies adversely affecting minorities. "Robertson is outspoken," said John Johnson, a writer for the *Cincinnati Enquirer,* "and can come across as somewhat brusque." Robertson commented, "I don't try to hurt anybody. But everyone says that my tongue is sharp."

Underground Railroad

Ever mindful of what African Americans had to endure and the need for education about slavery and racial discrimination, Robertson, who remains astonished that people could be so mean to others, and his wife, Yvonne, have taken a leadership role in what will be the National Underground Railroad Freedom Center.

The Underground Railroad was neither underground nor a railroad, but a nationwide network of locations and people, pre–Civil War, helping runaway slaves escape to safety. Due to open in 2004 on the banks of the Ohio River joining Cincinnati and northern Kentucky, the center will commemorate and honor both the escaped slaves who risked their lives to seek freedom and those who assisted the runaways and provided for their safe passage.

Giving of Himself

Robertson has worked with various youth, health, and civil rights organizations and other charitable endeavors, including the Boys and Girls Clubs of America, HOME (Housing Opportunities Made Equal), the National Association for the Advancement of Colored

NAACP executive director Benjamin Hooks *(far left)* poses with *(from left to right)* sportwriter Sam Lacy, former NBA star Sam Jones, baseball legend Hank Aaron, and Oscar Robertson after naming them to a sports advisory committee formed to improve minority practices among major sports franchises.

People (NAACP), the American Red Cross, and the American Cancer Society. He has served on the board of directors or been a spokesperson for many of them.

Among the many awards Robertson and his wife have received for their service is the Jewish National Fund's Tree of Life Award in 1992 for their professional and humanitarian leadership in their community.

The saying "Charity begins at home" really rang true in Robertson's life.

He and his wife, Yvonne, whom he met in college and married in 1970, have three daughters, Shana, Tia, and Mari. He was with Yvonne when she gave birth to Shana and Mari. But when Tia, the middle child, was born on January 10, 1964, Robertson was in Boston for the all-star game, in which he led the East to a 111–107 victory and emerged as MVP. Yvonne watched that game on television.

In 1989, Tia began developing symptoms of what would turn out to be lupus, a disease that causes the body's immune system to attack tissues and vital organs, often the kidneys. By 1994, doctors determined the disease was causing Tia's kidneys to fail, and decided by late 1996 that, for her to have a normal life, she would need a kidney transplant.

Tests of all members of the immediate family showed that her sister Shana and her father were the best candidates to donate a kidney. Robertson insisted that it was his responsibility. He didn't want Shana to go

through the procedure. He would be the best donor.

And in April 1997, at the age of fifty-eight, he did give one of his kidneys to Tia. "When you see a family member suffer, and you know there's a way out, you'd do almost anything to help," he said to John Johnson of the *Cincinnati Enquirer*.

After the six-hour procedure, Robertson asked, "How's Tia?" and then commented, "We were right, I was the best one to do this."

Oscar was overwhelmed by the outpouring of supportive messages and letters from strangers from around the country after the transplant.

"I think sometimes in life you're put here for a certain reason. Why are you living and breathing and someone else isn't? I don't think you're here just to mark time, even though you might not think that what you're doing is important."

He felt it was important that people learn about lupus and organ donation through his family's experience and, active with both the National Lupus Foundation and the National

Oscar Robertson at the zoo with his wife, Yvonne, and daughters Tia and Shana in September 1965.

Kidney Foundation, he has helped raise money for kidney and lupus research and become a national spokesperson for organ donation.

Teary-eyed at a news conference after the procedure, he said he was happy to have been able to donate the kidney to his daughter and would do it again, adding, "Parents do things every day for their kids. I'm not a hero, I'm just a father."

When Robertson won a 1999 Father of the Year award from the National Father's Day Council, he commented, "There are a lot of great fathers in the world, and a lot of great mothers, too, I'm happy to say. If I can represent them in accepting this award, I'll be happy to do so."

Building for Children

Robertson fills his post-athletics days with a variety of activities. He plays a little tennis and some golf, and dabbles in carpentry. "I fool around with woodwork. I have a woodshop, and while I'm not an accomplished carpenter, I build a few things," he said on NBA.com.

But building something more idealistic is often on his mind.

"I want to build something up for my kids, for the kids of my employees, and for kids I don't even know across the country," he said in accepting the Cincinnati Minority Supplier of the Year award, sponsored by the Cincinnati Minority Supplier Development Council, Inc.

"I believe in providing opportunities, but if an employee can't get the job done, there is no sense applying. It's important for children to go to school and get [good] grades," he told Gordon Engelhardt of the *Indianapolis Star*.

Turning to the subject of heroism, he continued, "Most children today are taught from television that a hero is the one hitting the homer, throwing the touchdown, running faster, being in the movies, or working on some scheme where you cheat people and come out with billions of dollars. If that's true, we are in bad shape."

Robertson told Engelhardt in 1992 that he'd changed his mind about athletes being role models for children. "I used to think we had a tremendous responsibility. I know how athletes

influence young people. Maybe parents should be role models. Some players just aren't very good role models. Just because a guy can kick a ball, throw a ball, or dunk a ball doesn't make him a good role model."

Yet at a panel at the NAACP convention the following year, he declared, "Black athletes have to understand the power that they have and use it positively. With all the problems that face youth today and the fact that, although unjustly, they are looked upon so highly by children, they should put their popularity to work. Just imagine the power Michael Jordan would have with teenagers."

Mark Green, executive director of the Cincinnati Minority Supplier Development Council, called Robertson "a role model for not just young black African Americans, but youths as a whole."

Young people would do well to choose as a role model Oscar Robertson who, perhaps drawing on his own experience, would urge those attending seminars, youth rallies, and

Oscar Robertson enjoys a light moment with Seyuki Hirooka, president and CEO of Sharp Electronics, before participating in a "legends" game at Madison Square Garden on March 19, 1994.

school meetings with the following words: "Don't complain about what has happened to you or is happening. Make the most of your opportunities and be the best you can be in life."

glossary

amateur   One who engages in an activity as a
   pastime rather than as a profession.

assist   A pass from one player to another
   that leads directly to a basket.

center   Usually the tallest player on a team's
   starting unit; the player most responsible
   for plays closest to the basket, including
   rebounding, scoring, and shot blocking.

court   The playing space for a basketball
   game, measuring ninety-four feet long;
   also called the floor.

demeanor   A person's behavior or outward
   manner toward others.

forward   One of two players flanking the
   center, usually on offense. Forwards play

close to the basket and must be good shooters and rebounders. They are usually taller than guards, but shorter than centers.

fundamentals   Of or relating to essential structure, function, or facts; basic skills and strategy.

guards   The two players who constitute the "back court." One, known as the "point guard," generally brings the ball up-court and directs the plays.

heroism   Heroic conduct; the qualities of a hero.

idealistic   The act of placing standards of perfection or excellence before practical considerations.

Ku Klux Klan   A post–Civil War "secret" society that advocates white supremacy; known to terrorize African Americans.

merger   The combining of two or more organizations.

MVP   Most valuable player, usually awarded at the All-Star game and the NBA Finals.

quota The maximum number or proportion, especially in persons that may be admitted to a place, event, nation, group, or institution.

racism The belief that some races are inherently better than others.

rebound To retrieve the ball as it comes from the rim or backboard, taking possession of it for either team.

rookie Player in his or her first professional season.

Underground Railroad A network of houses and other places that slavery opponents used to help slaves escape to freedom before the Civil War.

International Basketball Association
One Corporate Place
1501 42nd Street, Suite 371
West Des Moines, IA 50266
Web site: http://www.ibasketball.com

Naismith Memorial Basketball Hall of Fame
1150 West Columbus Avenue
Springfield, MA 01105
(413) 781-6500
(877) 4HOOPLA (446-6752)
Web site: http://www.hoophall.com or
    http://www.basketballhalloffame.com
The Web site of the Naismith Memorial
    Basketball Hall of Fame features
    biographies of all members of the Hall,
    along with news, events, information, and
    stories of basketball history.

Web Sites

The BigO.com

http://www.thebigo.com

ESPN

http://www.espn.com

Get updates about your favorite players and read sports-related articles.

National Basketball Association (NBA)

http://www.nba.com

A strong sports history Web site.

for further reading

Anderson, Dave. *The Story of Basketball.*
    Rev. ed. New York: William Morrow &
    Co., 1998.

Layden, Joseph. *NBA Slam-Dunk Champions.*
    New York: Scholastic, 1997.

Pluto, Terry. *Tall Tales: The Glory Years of
    the NBA.* Lincoln, NE: University of
    Nebraska Press, 2000.

Roberts, Randy. *But They Can't Beat Us:
    Oscar Robertson and the Crispus Attucks
    Tigers.* Champaign, IL: Sports Publishing,
    Inc, 1999.

Robertson, Oscar. *The Art of Basketball: A
    Guide to Self-Improvement in the
    Fundamentals of the Game.* Los Angeles:
    Oscar Robertson Media Ventures, 1998.

index

About the Author

Joel H. Cohen has written thirty-five books, most for young readers, and many of them with or about such athletes as Kareem Abdul-Jabbar, the Van Arsdale twins, Hank Aaron, Jim Palmer, Joe Morgan, Johnny Unitas, and Tom Seaver; entertainers Bill Cosby and Lucille Ball; author R. L. Stine; and illustrator Norman Rockwell. His articles have appeared in such publications as *TV Guide*, *Sports Illustrated for Kids*, *The New York Times*, and *Scholastic Scope*. He and his wife, Nancy, have four grown children and live in Staten Island, New York.

Acknowledgments

Special thanks to Larry Ridley, the National Basketball Association, the University of Cincinnati, and USA Basketball.

Photo Credits

Cover © Bettmann/Corbis; pp. 4, 8, 11, 18–19, 25, 30, 34, 37, 41, 48, 52–53, 58–59, 68, 75, 86–87, 94, 96 © Bettmann/Corbis; pp. 15, 45, 64, 82, 100 © AP/Wide World; pp. 90–91 © *Indianapolis Star*/AP Wide World.

Series Design and Layout

Geri Giordano